Impunity from Lunacy

Book One

by

Ellen Marie Blend

Dedication

I am dedicating this book to my dear friend, Charlie Brown, who devoted much of his life enlightening others about spiritual interactions and spreading words to heal the mind, body and spirit.

Charlie was born in Delta, Alabama, but had roots in Toledo, Ohio, where he ran the Heflin Printing Company, and also a newspaper called The Psychic Eye. The newspaper later became Body, Mind & Spirit News, followed by an on-line publication named Rev. Charlie Brown, after he retired in DeLand, Florida.

I would like to honor Charlie with this book, as he faithfully printed the many articles that I wrote from 2004 until his death in 2013. This book encompasses my articles published between those years and beyond.

Words of Witicism

For more than twenty years, Ellen Marie Blend has been connected with the spirit world. She receives messages and signs in various ways, but mainly in the mind's eye.

Her writings within are extrapolations of many sorts. She uses this quippy little verse to explain the origins of her work:

Anecdotes and Doze eh? Notes

Anecdote: A short narrative of an interesting, amusing, or biographical incident.

Doze: To sleep lightly; to be in a dull or stupefied condition.

*Eh: U*sed to ask for confirmation or repetition, or to express inquiry.

Note: To record or preserve in writing.

Her short articles are written after experiencing some noteworthy incidents, either via some sign or

---

Definitions from the Merriam-Webster dictionary.

while in a meditative state, which is sort of like dozing. She sometimes questions the information given her (eh?, an expression more commonly spoken by Canadians) because she has difficulty interpreting the message or cannot believe what she sees.

Other times, because the spirit world understands that she is slow to grasp things, they present the same information to her more than once to make sure that she gets it. She then takes to writing notes of her many experiences until they form a brief narrative.

While some topics are very touching and serious, others may make one raise an eyebrow in question of their validity. Rather than be offended by those who disbelieve her, she chose to present this compendium of articles in a fashion that interjects some cartoon humor and can be enjoyed by all who seek this information.

She chose to present her articles alphabetically rather than in chronological order. Her free verse poetry is noted in italics.

Alphabetical Listing of Articles and Poems

A Lucky Penny

If you think your guardian angel is not watching over you, think again. One of mine has a way of letting me know she is there. I call her my "money angel," as she has always made sure that I had just enough money.

My girlfriend, Stephanie, and I take an annual shopping trip to London, Ontario, to celebrate her birthday. She likes to drive, and has a great natural awareness of where she is and where to go. I, contrarily, do not enjoy driving, and without a sense of direction, never know where I am. She would have to direct me every step of the way, so it makes sense for her to drive on such a long journey. Furthermore, she is able to carry on a conversation and read a road map all while driving. She tells me that her idea of relaxation is to get in her car and drive.

At the time of this writing, her car has about 285,000 miles on it and needs a few items repaired. Mechanically, the car is always taken care of, but it gets a lot of use as she travels for work. She often drives to other states with her car.

I sat down in the passenger seat. As we began our journey, it felt as though the wheels of the car were loose and would literally roll off the car. Her passenger-side mirror has been missing for some time, and the window on the same side has been stuck in the open position, about three inches down; it has been taped shut to allow no air in the car.

Although the car is a bright yellow color, it has been speckled with black road tar ever since I can remember. The hinges on the driver side door finally gave way, and the door would fly open when she would make a left-hand turn. She has since had the door fixed, but she claims it is the best car she has ever owned.

As we ventured down the highway and onto the freeway, I silently prayed that we would make it there and back safely on our journey. If we were to get stranded in another country, I could not imagine our cost to get back to the U.S.

We pulled into the customs' office lot, and Stephanie parked her car. We had stopped to exchange some American money for Canadian before crossing the bridge to Canada. As I opened my car door, there was a bright, shiny penny on the ground. I knew it was there for me, as my money angel has often gifted me with a sign such as this. I picked it up, and thoughtfully put it in my handbag, thanking her and the heavens for this sign. I now knew that I could relax and our trip would be made safely.

A Matter of
Independent Thinking

I had been reading the second book in a series that heavily supported The Course in Miracles. I found it highly repetitive, like brainwashing, but for the purpose of drilling in the hard to accept material. Being an open minded person, I could rationalize most of its contents. However, my doubting mind was still at work when I went to bed.

I could sense the presence of spirits around me by the light activity going on in my internal vision. So, I asked the question, "Is there any validity to the material that is within that book?"

Suddenly a nickel was thrust forward, then receded, several times in a row. I could see a head on the face of the nickel and quickly thought it was George Washington. "I cannot tell a lie," ran through my mind, and then I corrected my thoughts to say, "No, George Washington is on the quarter."

In the morning I searched for a nickel and found the face of Thomas Jefferson and the word liberty. He was noted for The Declaration of Independence. "Oh," I surmised, "It is up to the individual as to what he or she chooses to believe. We have that liberty."

Liberty

A Romantic Kiss

Some may think that your guides don't know what you're thinking, but I can assure you that they do.

When watching television, I occasionally see a romantic scene where a couple is totally engaged in kissing. They are so passionate with one another.

One evening, after having gone to bed, one of my guides paid me a visit in my internal vision. I could sense that he was speaking to me in an endearing manner. Then his face appeared more clearly, and besides his fair complexion, I saw a straight, nicely trimmed mustache above his upper lip. It was quite distinguishing, I might add, and I was now facing him.

My hair was pulled back away from my face and was styled in large folds of curls on the back of my head. It was a natural shade of blonde, not the color of my hair in this lifetime. Then this man placed his hands on both sides of my face, drawing me near him, and gave me the most romantic kiss!

The vision was then over, and I've rationalized that one of my guides had been my lover in a previous life. He was letting me know that I had experienced a passion with him that I sometimes see in the movies. It was a fulfilling encounter to realize that

I had been loved like that, and maybe still am. Perhaps he has been a guide through many lifetimes.

Ryzhov Sergey

A Soul Mate's Visit

It was ten years since she had seen her soul mate. They had agreed to part based on a karmic debt that had called him due. It was only intended that a limited break take place in the relationship, but now many years had elapsed and each had their own course in life plotted.

Over the years each had encountered other love affairs, not lasting, but meaningful nonetheless. Neither she nor her soul mate sought to rekindle their relationship, a love that had lasted through many lifetimes. Still now, that love burned strong, but they were on different paths.

A psychic reader had told her that his and another's spirit would collide, and that re-consummation of their relationship would not be right for her now. Another soul would be sent to her to make that new perfect union. She waited.

One evening her soul mate came to her in a hazy, life-like dream. He was seeking reconfirmation of their love and what it was that he should do. Should he step out of the way of that other soul? "You are the love of my life," she told him with great emotion. He felt peace and cried. He was satisfied that their love was eternal, then vanished.

A Time of Change

I have two children, a son and daughter. My daughter lived with me prior to her getting married, and I developed a closer relationship to her than to my son. My son had a better connection with his dad as they worked together in business and spent much time together at home.

The business that my son and his father had failed, and they both were losing everything. My son was losing his house in bankruptcy. Eviction notices were arriving frequently, and he was busily looking for another place to live. I accompanied him several times to comfort him, and to give him parental support as needed. I was soon to experience a change in my life due to this.

In his looking, I found a house that piqued my interest, although I hadn't planned on moving. This particular house had some attributes that were better than my current home, and the property also had an additional building that could easily be made into another home, one which my son could renovate and use for himself.

We both saw the attractiveness to this idea, and I made an offer to purchase the property. It was at this time that my son realized that I was truly there to support him in his time of need. That is when the change really began to take place.

I was in the real estate office signing the papers, and found a quarter on the floor. I walked across a parking lot and found change on the ground. I went to a funeral home and found a dime on the chair. In shopping, I found change at the curb walking from the parking lot to the store.

Money was appearing so frequently, that while at a fast food drive thru, I pulled up to the window and opened the car door. I looked down at the pavement, and there was change on the ground as I knew there would be. I found that there was money everywhere for me.

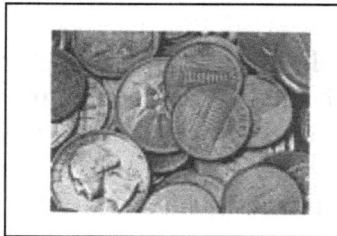

There was never very much money, perhaps a nickel or a dime, but mostly pennies. I knew that they were there for me, for there were far too many occurrences for them to be there by chance. The message was that "there was going to be a lot of change in my life." My son now knew that he could count on me.

I had put my house up for sale, and the purchase of the new home was contingent upon the sale of my current home. Before the sale could be consummated, another offer was made on the home I was to buy, without a contingency. That meant that I either had to complete the sale with a bridge loan, or back out on the deal.

As it turned out, I became very uncomfortable about moving to the new location, and I sensed that my son was also uncertain about the great distance he would have to travel to a new job. I let the house go, and the events that followed gave us both peace of mind. I also learned that a significant amount of "change" had been made in my life.

Akashic Records

The Akashic Records are known as "The Book of Life," and are said to be a vibrational record and contain the entire history, thought, word, experience and future possibilities of every soul.

Frits Ahlefeldt

I met a gal at a social event who was quite charming, but still suffering from both the loss of her son and husband, in consecutive years. She was trying to understand why they were both taken from her, and why so close together.

"I suppose it was just meant to be," she said. We talked about spirituality, and about the Akashic Records. She said she could almost accept her husband's death, but not that of a young child. I agreed that his death was predestined, and part of the Akashic Records.

That night when I went to bed, thoughts still lingering on her sadness, I saw the Akashic Records in my mind's eye. A guide was telling me that, indeed, the young man's death had been pre-established.

A light green light overshadowed the wall of records. It appeared as if there were file sections cut into the wall, each about 9" x 14". I was shown writing across the wall, on particular file sections, in a cursive style. It was not an American cursive writing that I could read. It was illegible, as if from another time period.

I tried to research the earliest cursive handwriting, which I traced back to the 17th century, but could not find anything that resembled what I saw on the Akashic wall. By my guide showing me the Akashic wall, I was able to confirm that the young man's dying was part of his pre-destined fate.

Perhaps the writing was just a symbolic representation, showing me visually that the young man's death was a matter of record.

Alien Visit

At his moment, I would still question if I actually had a visit from a friendly little Alien or just a dream.

My visitor had an Alien head and body, and her face was visibly female. She was a young girl, green in color, and her body thinned to a mere tail.

Christos Georghiou
(modified)

She had the warmest expression, and I welcomed her as a friendly spirit.

The rest of the visit was some explanation of the eight levels of her existence, which were shown as thin sheets in a file tray. Picture a desk tray with many level separators. She was trying to explain these eight levels, as she moved about freely, but I was left not understanding what these were.

Her departure was as warm as her entrance, and it has left me wondering. Since I am a visionary, I receive much information while in a hazy state of meditation. I'm therefore inclined to believe that she actually did visit me, and that she presented herself to me through a dream.

Angel of Protection

I had a perfectly good car, but I had always admired one of the more luxurious, higher echelon cars on the market. They were, of course, unaffordable, but I always told myself that someday I would have one.

Then one day, while driving on a major thoroughfare, with numerous shops, restaurants and businesses on either side, one of my desired cars was parked out front on a used car lot. It was a small BMW, in a beautiful shade of blue with a blue convertible top. While I never turn back when I've missed something, this time I did. I looked the car over, and wrote down the name and number of the dealership.

I made an inquiry about the car when I got home, to find that because it was used, it was within my buying range. After some negotiation, I purchased the car. I also thought, "If you tell God often enough that you really want something, he makes it available to you."

Next I had to decide how to sell my current car. It was not a very good time to sell a used vehicle, as car dealerships were offering incredible 0% financing on new vehicles. So, I decided to put a sign in the car window and to drive it one evening to get some visibility.   After stopping for gas, I pulled out of the station and into the lane to get onto the freeway.   I checked for oncoming traffic, and finding none, began my left- hand turn.

While making that turn, a car came up over a hill toward me without giving me enough time to get out of the way. My car was hit in the passenger door.   I felt like I saw stars, and found myself floating, in silence, with the help of the airbags. I was carefully lifted into the air and reseated as I brought the car to a full stop. No one was hurt in the accident at all, but I had the strangest feeling that the accident had been orchestrated in order for me to be rid of the car.

A policeman who had come to the scene of the accident drove me home, as my car was not drivable. However, I was still astonished at how easily I was able to walk away from the accident unhurt.   I am certain that my carefully being lifted into the air and being reseated again was an angel experience, an angel of protection.

Angels Abound

Ever since I made my plea to see an angel, I have been given many opportunities to be aware that they are plentiful and around me.

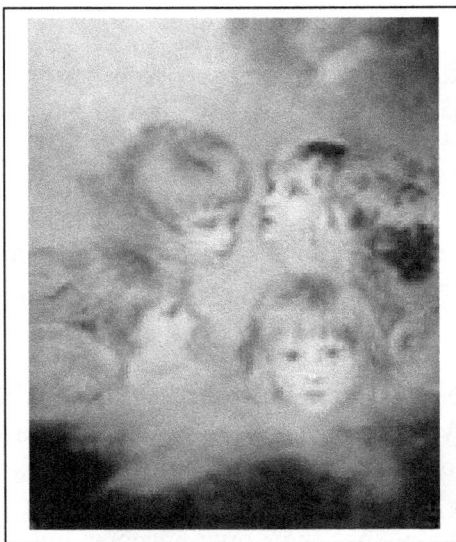

One evening, when lying down to sleep, my internal vision was covered with a soft, lavender and white veil, that I could only explain as being feathered. While I was enthralled and captivated with this sight, another entered my viewing screen in pink, with the same wispy, delicate covering.

Angels, I confirmed to myself. Angels are around me in soft pastels. I wonder why not powder blue. Then I remembered reading that angels have different colored wings and tips. I looked in the book I have about angels and found that the lavender was probably one of the Thrones, and the pink, Cherubim or Seraphim, both joyous singers, although I heard no music.

Not more than a couple of nights following, I was again blessed with angels. My first sight was of emerald green, with a bright gold, clearly the Powers and Principalities, neither of whom were in pastel. Then, as an answer to my request, I was shown the wings of white and powder blue, perhaps one of the Virtues, and then aqua, most definitely an Archangel.

Then, the most beautiful angel appeared, looking at me from above. She had long, lovely dark hair, and the prettiest, delicate features on her pleasant face.

Each of the angels has their own purpose, but to me it was their way of teaching that they are present. Because of my ability to see them, I can convey to you of their existence.

Antioch, Antioch, Where Art Thou?

Each time I went into the bathroom, either to use the facilities, comb my hair, or put on makeup, an invisible spirit guide repeatedly said, "Antioch." The word played over and over in my mind, but it was never audible. No message followed, and there was no vision to help me identify what Antioch was to mean.

I mentioned this to my friend, Gwenn, and she said she pictured an Indian Chief by the name of Antioch.

I looked Antioch up in the dictionary and found it to be an ancient city in Turkey. This did not give me any clues to my recurring message. For days, I still was reminded of Antioch each time I entered that bathroom.

I kept asking for more information, and finally I got small clues. I got the feeling of "things being rolled out."

A few days later, I received another clue. The word "naïve" came in, and I related it to one of the lower levels of an archeological system. I also looked up "naïve", finding it to be "next in order, or next to nothing, a point, or tip."

A new clue was more visual. In my mind's eye, I was presented with a triangular paper model, origami, that constantly "popped" as it sprung back to shape after being depressed. I was to surmise, "small things of unimportance would be popping up." I later learned that my interpretation was incorrect.

I went to lunch and met several girls with whom I used to work. One of them told me of her excitement of buying a new cottage, and that she and her husband would be going there that weekend. "Oh, I said, where is your cottage?"

"Antioch," she said.

I got on the Internet when I got home and did a search for "Antioch," finding it was located near Cadillac, Michigan. I also found that there was a church of Antioch and an email address.

I wrote to the church of Antioch and asked them if they could tell me what Antioch meant in their church name. They kindly replied and said that it was named after the city in Turkey where it was believed that people were first called Christians.

A few days later, my friend, Gwenn, called me. "I have a message for you," she said.

"Oh, what's that?" I asked.

"Well, our friend, Shannon, went to a wedding Saturday which was held at a hall and not a church, and the priest that came to marry the couple was from the Church of Antioch. Just passing the message along," she said.

I was totally perplexed at why this message kept coming to me, and I could not resolve why. It was a couple of years later that I realized that my deceased agent had died of cancer in the city of Antioch, and someone in the spiritual world was trying to let me know of his failing health and ultimate death.

Barbara

Barbara had tried to reach me a couple of times throughout the day, but I was too busy. I sensed that she was trying to get through, but I did not take the time to find out what it was that she wanted. My subconscious mind was very much aware of her, but my conscious mind was not.

Her daughter had just read my tarot cards and spoke of the strained relationship she had always had with her psychic mother. She was grateful to her, however, for teaching her the art of the Tarot. Both were gifted and actively reading cards for people.

When I went to bed that night, Barbara again approached me. I closed my eyes as I spoke to her. "Oh, yes," I said, now acknowledging her. "You were trying to reach me all day, weren't you!"

A circle of white light appeared, and I stared at its brightness. Now the circle became the entire white screen of my vision. My reaction was: "Oh no, a blank screen!" I hated blank screens, for that usually meant that no more information was forthcoming.

Barbara must have heard my thoughts; she scattered brown speckles across the white background of my visual screen. Then angelic white lighters appeared.

I could not see her, but I sensed that she was there. I watched the white lighters as they gathered around.

No information followed; however, she was showing me that she came to me directly from the white light of God. Perhaps I was to relay a message to her daughter that she had been misunderstood and meant only good things for her, I thought.

I watched the white lighters for some time, and then a crack appeared in the corner of a wall in my vision. The wall began to open at the bottom, and then the floor tilted.

"What does that mean, Barbara?" I asked. "Can you be more specific? I can't interpret that."

I really didn't expect an answer. Normally when I asked for more information, another picture would be presented that still needed interpretation. Nothing happened. Then I heard Barbara speak. It was a deep voice, and she said, "This is where I must go; I cannot remain."

I understood then that she had entered through a portal, and would leave the same way. Now nothing appeared in my internal vision, but I could still hear her talking in the background. Her voice was distinctively deep, but not audible, as she was

not talking to me. Then there was silence, and I
went to sleep for the night.

Carried Forward

Among the many attributes I acquired from my parents, there are a few that have carried forward from one or more lifetimes. Through self regression and past-life recall, I have found that I have lived with my same family members more than once. I confirmed this through some extraordinary revelations while traveling in England, as cited in my book, "Looking Back."

Although memories of my past lives are not limited to England, they seem to be more easily recalled as they took place in more recent years. Of course, I was in England when much information was given to me by my spirit guides.

The experience of this recall and the recognition of the land that I had never seen in this lifetime was astounding. More and more information was presented to me with the exposure to the ground that I was visiting. I was given excerpts of different lifetimes, pieces of conversations from parents, and was left to put all of the pieces together.

Now that I have visited the land and experienced the culture there, I am more aware of the notable words that have carried forward from my past lives in England. When receiving a greeting of "hi" from someone, I respond with "hello." I also have always spelled the color gray "grey," just as the English do, and prefer writing theatre to theater.

My British friend, Duncan, who escorted me through England, confirmed this, and has told me that he has noticed many things that I do and say that are definitely of English culture.

Clearing Entities

With things that had been going in my life, I felt strongly that I must still have a karmic debt that needed to be paid.

I went to a tarot card reader and, without mentioning my concerns, she offered emphatically that my karma had been completed. My question to the universe was answered.

On my spiritual journey, I continually looked for information that would educate me and also help other people. I was always looking for ways to assist others, as I coached many and provided healing information when appropriate.

My friend Gwenn's life had been so bleak, and she definitely needed assistance. I took her to a channeler for help. This was the first time that I heard about an Entity Release. Gwenn was quite receptive about following through with any spiritual guidance, and I hoped that it would help her.

I read the Entity Release for myself a few times over the last several years trying to get relief for my own situation, but nothing was ever felt, and no improvement was made. My situation stayed the same.

I continually looked up information on the Internet regarding the angels that assist Archangel Michael in the Entity Release, as I knew nothing about them. I studied whatever information I could find.

I came upon healing mantras and encountered a posting that said that it has been discovered that the field entity release would not deal with trespassers within the Circle itself; therefore another version had been developed. This version addressed the Keepers of the Circle and instructed that my job was to keep sending love and continuous honor to the Keepers.

I no sooner began to ask Ariel, K'or Takh, and Grace, Purity, Mercy, Rapture and Liberty Elohim to enter my Circle from the Legacy, and I could feel exactly what was said would happen: I felt the expansion of the presence of these beings within the Circle.

As instructed, I asked them to remove any entities, dark forces, or alien observers from my Circle. The posting said that I may hear conversation coming from the Circle and I did. It also said that I may feel many emotions running through me, that they were most likely from the entities, but may be from the Keepers. I felt busyness going on. It said that I may feel a "thank you" coming from the Keepers when it was complete. I did.

I was also told to set up a Triple Grid to keep areas like my home energetically clean. As advised, I used a spherical object, a crystal (glass) ball. When finished, I sealed the grids, and thought I was done.

It was a short time later that a depression came all over me. I understood that it was from grief described as one of the emotions I might feel from the intruders, but I was still astonished. I expected that some entities had stayed behind and not left the circle.

I repeated the entire set of protections again, asking for Archangel Michael to bring down the tunnel of light and proceeded once again to do the Entity Release. I then asked for the Keepers of the Circle to assist, and performed the entire ritual again, and followed up with the Triple Grid protection. I felt safer the remainder of the day.

The following day I still felt that I was not totally protected, and as instructed said "Renew Grid," while holding on to my spherical ball. I felt, however, that I was still not clear of the entities. I reprogrammed the ball with the Triple Grid again. Since then, I have felt free and unbothered, and my hopes are that a healing shall begin.

Crème in Your Coffee?

One afternoon when I had a few moments to rest, I laid down on the couch. Thoughts of family members must have been on my mind, and I remember thinking about my late grandfather.

Soon a vision of a young woman, perhaps in her late twenties to early thirties, appeared. She had long, dark blonde hair, and was talking to someone. I so clearly made out her features and watched the movement of her mouth as she spoke.

She was in conversation with an adult, but I could not see that person. She was holding a small baby boy in her arms. I did not feel that it was my grandfather, but it may have been one of his brothers. I sensed that this woman was my grandfather's mother.

I knew nothing about her and have never even seen a picture of her. I doubt that one ever existed in my immediate family. My grandfather had been orphaned by the death of both of his parents at a young age. They died of either diphtheria or scarlet fever. All of the children were taken in by neighbors to be raised with children of their own. My grandfather was raised by a French family.

The clarity in which I saw this woman was intense. The movement of her mouth, the exactness of her features and facial expressions made me feel that I should know her well, but I did not. She most definitely bore the resemblance of her offspring, my grandfather.

The vision left me, but I dearly wanted to see more of her. My request was immediately granted, and this time I paid more attention to her hair and clothing. She had neat, long, medium blonde hair, that laid upon her shoulders. She was wearing a dress and now was walking down the street on a sidewalk. It was like watching a moving picture.

I described her dress as having been crème colored. I repeated the word with this spelling as I continued to write. I knew very well that the color was spelled c-r-e-a-m, like the cream in your coffee, but I was subconsciously insistent upon spelling it c-r-e-m-e. Months later, still knowing this, I was still unwilling to change the spelling. I described her dress as follows.

The dress had gathered, short sleeves, a tight bodice and a moderately full skirt. Its color was crème with black detail. There was black ribbon, or some other detail, like piping, on the bodice of the dress, while the sleeves were a solid crème. The skirt had some vertical-lined design broken by an occasional flower crossing it on the crème-colored background.

This vision was so vivid that I felt I had somehow been there with her and could see how she looked, acted and felt. It was some time later that I realized that the reason I was so resolute on that spelling of c-r-e-m-e was because she was French. The spirit world was giving me one more piece of information about this woman that I never knew.

Dark Eyes

A lot of good things had been happening for me, and I was quite appreciative. I thanked God for my good fortune many times, and for the happiness that had been given to me.

One night after I had gone to bed, I had a visitor. I often have visitors of spiritual entities or guides after retiring for the evening. Sometimes my visitors are shown in the form of physical beings that I do not know. This time, and not his first appearance to me, I was startled to find Jesus come into plain view.

As before, he appeared to rise up into my mental vision with utmost clarity. Others just seem to manifest themselves into view, but Jesus actually rises up into view. "Jesus, is that you?" I questioned. "It is you, isn't it!" I exclaimed.

He allowed me to look directly at his face and into his eyes for a short time. Among his other distinct features, I noticed his very dark eyes, and within them I saw deep feeling. He then turned his face sideways and allowed me to look at him more closely. He held his place there for a long moment before disappearing.

I questioned why I was to have such a visit, and reasoned that it must have been his way of letting me know that he received the thanks that I sent to him. I also questioned if I should claim that I knew of his dark eyes, and was soon sent confirmation by a picture which was included in an email.

Digging up Synchronicity

A friend of mine sells real estate, and his customer wanted a piece of commercial property with a building on it to operate a business. The customer was shown a property having the right specifications and an adjoining piece of vacant land, both of which she wanted to purchase. Because the properties were located far away from her residence, she also wanted to move closer to her new place of business and bought a residential property through my friend as well.

The seller of the commercial properties said that the closing would have to wait until he returned home as he was doing a job out of town. My agent friend said that was fine, because his uncle had died and he would be going to the funeral up north.

In conversation, the seller said that he would have to finish digging the holes before he could go home. The agent assumed he must be digging fence post holes, but asked him anyway. "No," the gentleman replied. "Grave site holes. I'm in West Branch, Michigan, and that's a long way from home."

"West Branch!" my friend exclaimed. "That's where I'm going for my uncle's funeral."

They confirmed that the cemetery where the man was digging holes was the same as where the uncle was going to be buried, and then the seller asked what the uncle's name was. When my agent friend told him, he said, "Well, I'm digging his grave right now!"

My agent friend is certain that his deceased uncle orchestrated the three sales to remember him by. "A triple sale like that does not happen that easily in this business," he said.

Nilikha

Dream Answer

A friend dropped me an email. She said, "I meant to write to you on Sunday. I had a dream about you Saturday night. It was a pleasant dream and you were sitting in a lovely room with lots of windows, reading a book. You looked very peaceful, like you were really enjoying the book. That's it!! I didn't talk to you; I just saw you in the room.

What do you make of this? Or am I just crazy?"

I returned her message saying, "No, you're not crazy--you're psychic! I have been editing one of my books and reliving a true love story about my relationship with Mike. I have been deliberately sitting in my living room by the doorwall to get the sunshine. You saw it correctly!!! You must have mentally asked the question, "I wonder what Ellen is up to" and got your answer in the dream!

Eighty-Nine Cents

My husband and I were headed for the casino. I speak of my Money Angel frequently, and I think everyone who gambles must wish for one. I don't care to gamble, but my husband finds it a great source of entertainment with its accompanying excitement of the chance that you could win.

As we were walking to the casino from the parking lot, when approaching the driveway in front of the main entrance, I spotted a great deal of change on the pavement. Sixty-four cents was found and picked up by me as quickly as I could. I privately thought that my Money Angel was there and giving me a sign.

The available slot machines were plentiful, and my husband was having his usual day of accumulated small losses. We decided to take a break and enjoy a beverage at the bar. As I was walking on the carpeted entrance to the lounge, a bright shiny quarter was on the floor. I stopped to pick it up, "Hmm, I thought. She's still watching."

Normally the change I find is only a penny here and a penny there. I never ask or expect my Money Angel to protect us from losses or provide any gains, but I am always pleased when I know she is present. This particular day she was being especially generous as she had provided a total of 89 cents.

We decided to give the slot machines a last try before leaving, which proved to be fruitful. My husband was able to regain all of his losses, and leave with a proud small profit to make his day. It was about 89 dollars. I can only presume that we had some divine assistance.

Energy Force

Spirits abound, I know;
they are with us always.
I do not live alone;
they surround me,
though only one is listed
at my residence and it is I.

When I lie in bed at night,
they come to me.
When I ask them,
they answer my questions.

I don't always understand
their message,
but I am satisfied
that they are there.

During the day,
I busily trod through the house
doing my chores,
perhaps dusting, making the
bed, putting clothes away—
and find that I have walked
through a powerful energy.

It surrounds me
with a whirl of cool air
and I know that
I have just walked
through their space.

I felt the energy force;
but they are busy, too,
and did not get out of my way.

Facing North

"I have stories I could tell you!," a lady commented when seeing a number of my paranormal books for sale at a counter. "When my mother died, there were three of us children left, and we each were asked to throw a red rose upon her casket before she was buried. When she was alive, she always had to sleep with her head facing north. Even when she traveled, she would be careful to select a room where she could face that way when she slept."

The lady continued, "When we were at her grave, and had each thrown a rose upon her casket, a voice was heard. The voice said, 'Is the head facing north?' No one admitted to having said those words, and we can only believe that she asked that question herself."

I had certainly heard that the spirit can manifest itself in several ways after passing. This was to give proof.

My friend, Gwenn, has told me that there is truth for the need for some to have their head facing north when they sleep. She said it is because of the strength of one's magnetic field.

Before their mother was lowered into the grave, the funeral director assured them that their mother's head was definitely facing north. The family members knew it had better be, or their mother would never rest in peace.

Fairy Dust

After a hard day's work,
I am anxious to get to bed
and to sleep.
I pull the covers back, get into
bed, and close my tired eyes.

Sparkles of fairy dust appear
before my closed eyes.
I open my eyes,
and the sparkles disappear.

I close them again and see
the fairy dust you sprinkle,
and I admire the beauty of you,
sweet fairy.

I am comforted to know
that you are with me.
I have seen you in my mind's
eye to know that you are there.

51

Get Going

While I lie sleeping, a bright light awakened me. I found myself speedily driving down well-marked roads and watching the white and yellow lines fly by me. I turned right, then left, stopped at a stop sign, and then continued driving. I saw yellow road signs, speed limit signs, and continued to make my turns as I raced through the city.

When I was fully awake, I mused over the exercise I'd just been through. I tried to figure out why this little scenario took place.

I had some concerns about the drive I was to take that day. In fact, I had to leave the house within a couple of hours of waking to pick up two ladies who were to accompany me to my future daughter-in-law's bridal shower. The location of the shower was about forty minutes from my home.

My guiding spirit must have been excited about the event, and wanted me to get up and get going so that I could pick up the girls.

Ghost in the House

I was having an addition built onto my home, and the builder and I often engaged in conversation while he worked. He was aware that I spent much of my time writing. "What do you write about," he had asked. I told him that much of my writing was about metaphysical things that happened in my life. "Paranormal happenings," I offered.

"Well," he said, "When I first bought my current home, there was a ghost that lived there. My wife and I could hear noises in the house. One day we both heard a crashing noise upstairs, like broken glass, or a broken mirror. We rushed upstairs to see what had happened but found nothing."

"How very interesting," I said.

He continued, "Another time, my wife was upstairs and heard someone downstairs in the house. She presumed it was me, and that I had come home from work for something. When she went downstairs to find me, she found my office light on, but I was not there.

Later that evening, when I returned home, she asked what I had come home for earlier. I told her I hadn't. She then exclaimed she had heard someone walk around, and she knew the office light was off when she had gone upstairs."

"You don't hear those noises or find signs anymore?" I asked.

"Actually, no," he said. "It has all stopped. I don't know why that is, but we're not bothered by it anymore."

Antimartina

Green Light – Go

In reading a recent horoscope, I was told that I needed to complete a statement in regard to what it was that I produced naturally. I related it to my interests in the spiritual world and the products of writing that I produced.

The horoscope further stated that I would not be able to progress into my next evolutionary stage until I had completed this statement. I wondered if my next phase might be in the area of healing.

Without putting it into words, I mentally asked the spiritual world, as I often did during my meditative moments, just what was meant by this statement. In essence I said, "Is it all right for me to ask you what it is that I am supposed to do?"

Normally I would receive some sort of white light to let me know that someone was there. This time I got a green light, meaning "Go – ask your question." When I did, my face began to feel very warm, just as the warmth felt by a healer. I then knew that my next phase would be in healing.

Gremlin

I was awakened from my lying position on the couch by a spiritual entity who moved my feet in order to sit down. I could physically see his short little body with outstretched legs in a transparent form. He cajoled himself by playing an imaginary musical instrument while singing ta-tat-ta-tat-ta-ta.

I described this little creature to my friend, Gwenn. "He was an ugly little man," I said, "with short legs."

"That was your Gremlin," she said. "Your spirits must have been down at some point recently."

"If they were, I didn't realize it," I said, "but maybe I had been feeling a little low."

"Well, that's when Gremlins appear in your life, when your spirits are low," she confirmed.

This little Gremlin tantalized me for the entire year by running my boat battery and car battery down several times. In my car, I would find my trunk left open, the interior light on, or maybe the glove box door open, all leaving a light on in the car to run the battery down. I don't have such careless habits, so to have this happen so regularly, it was clear that there was some meddling going on.

He also fooled with the operation of the light in my office, causing it to work intermittently. He froze the television programming, and created havoc with other electrical things around the house.

When I tried to tell my son about my Gremlin messing with my computer, he said, "Mom, everyone has a computer Gremlin!"

Greta

I attended a psychic class wherein the teacher put each of the students in touch with a spirit guide. When it came to my turn, I was told that a very peasant looking woman was coming forward, and hat she wasn't very spiritual. I was told that she was there to see that I took care of myself.

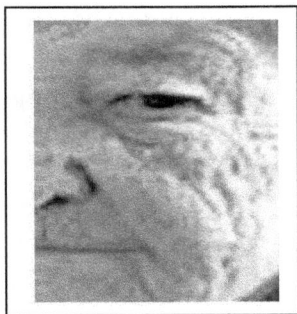

Greta

The instructor also told me that she carried a rolling pin and, when she saw that I wasn't taking care of myself, she would nudge me with it. She also said that my guide wanted to be called Greta.

A few nights passed, and one evening after I had gone to bed, a bright light appeared before my closed eyes. I opened them to find that the room was completely dark. I closed them again and the light reappeared.

There was a large circle of light wherein a very old woman appeared showing only one side of her face. Her skin was quite wrinkled and she did not smile. Greta had merely come to introduce herself.

The next day I was making a second pot of coffee and was reusing the same filter, as it had stuck in the holder instead of coming out with the used grounds. I figured it was still fresh enough to be reused. As I reached for the coffee canister, my hand brushed against the cabinet door and it stung with excruciating pain, much more than could possibly be caused by my mere brushing against the wood. Greta, in her non-spiritual way, had whacked me with her rolling pin!

Guardian Angel

I had asked to tag along on a small trip that my pilot son, Gary, and his girlfriend, Eileen, were taking to visit her relatives in Muskegon. They would be flying out Saturday and returning Sunday in a four-seater Cessna. I wanted to visit one my friends in that area while they visited with her family. Eileen had flown with Gary previously, and was quite confident in his abilities.

Except for strong head winds, there was absolutely no problem with the flight. I had closed my eyes to rest on the flight there.

Having an extraordinary special connection with the spirit world, I saw someone in my mind's eye who looked very much like my higher self come forth. She was there to assure me of her presence and of our safety on the flight.

From what I understand, my higher self is me in the ethereal. She had presented herself in a full close-up, face-to-face view. When I acknowledged her, she backed away, allowing me to clearly see Jesus facing an alter in a clouded background.

Haunted Hatheway House
of New Baltimore, MI

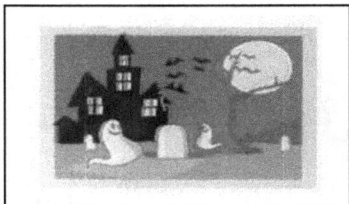

As a member of a local Writer's Group, I met a young lady who also wrote material of a paranormal nature. She told me about the Hatheway House nearby that had a history of strange happenings and extraordinary ghostly stories. The family who had lived there was very wealthy and prominent in New Baltimore. I had no knowledge of such a place, and she offered to drive me there as she was sure I would get some psychic information from this experience.

My author friend had heard a story that Gilbert Hatheway had a daughter, Mabel, who died at the age of 20 from mysterious causes. She had married a young man, without her father's approval, and came back to visit. Some say she was thrown down the stairs to her death.

Hatheway House

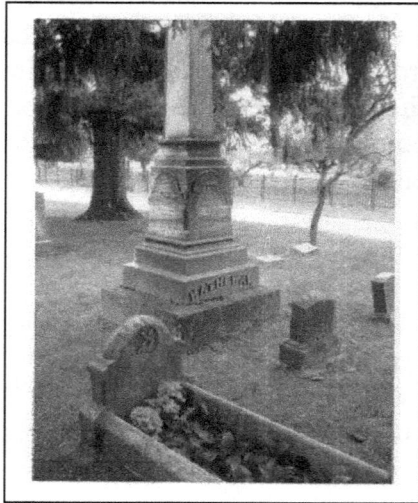

Hatheway Gravesites

It was a bright, sunny day, and we pulled up to the house on the corner of 24 Mile Road and Washington. It was a large Victorian home with two stories and a cupola at the top.

To her disappointment, and mine, I was unmoved at this viewing. However, that evening, when I retired to bed, I was given much information about this house in my mind's eye.

History of the Hatheway House
New Baltimore, Michigan

The house was built in the 1800's by Gilbert Hatheway, a smart New England businessman who came to New Baltimore to capitalize on shipping in the Great Lakes. According to accounts he was a stern man, with a strong sense of tradition.

He was also a philanthropist; he shared his wealth with the community and became a welcome fixture in this growing town which was the halfway point between Port Huron and Detroit.

According to the legends, Gilbert had a daughter named Mabel who met a young man named Oren from Paw Paw, a town on the west side of the state, now famous for its grape harvest and wineries.

Gilbert Hatheway disapproved and made his disapproval known. Still, headstrong, Mabel went ahead and married in November of 1833. She died the following March, and some say the circumstances of her death were mysterious. One legend was that she fell down the stairs of the mansion and broke her neck.

Eventually the Hatheways left the old house and it passed through several hands, becoming a bed and breakfast and later a rest home or sanitorium. Through the years people began to claim to hear things within the structure and to see shapes or forms.

The family is buried in the nearby cemetery.

This is the psychic information that I received:

Black, billowy clouds formed outside the home as I looked upon the two second-level windows. A beast with large arms reached out of the windows, with the head coming through the brick wall; it may have had a human face, but was definitely beastly.

I was shown a red card, a King of hearts or diamonds. Ripples ran through the King's back.

A lovely rich wood banister formed a landing across the upstairs, with a staircase descending on the right. A white, wispy entity swept through the halls and down the stairs.

There was much evil activity within the house— high winds, rocking, breaking of things, shaking of the walls, and fast, violent action. I saw wild, primary colors, and heard noise of an arcade and juke box.

From the second level, someone threw a doll down the stairs with great force, breaking it. It's arm fell off.

A few days later, I had another vision about the inhabitants of the house, but not significant to any hauntings.

I could see a man in a dark suit sitting at an old typewriter. He was on an upper level of the home. The typewritten page showed 12 pt. courier type. There were words crossed out, and editing marks on the page. There was also a woman upstairs, standing next to him.

Both the man and woman were fair skinned. The man had a distinguished mustache with the ends turned down. The woman was approximately 35 to 40 years old and was wearing a black dress with a white apron and either a nurse's or maid's hat. The man was in the same age range.

Gilbert was said to be terribly arthritic, and probably had a maid or nurse on staff to assist him.

I Heard Her Voice

A few days after I purchased a book on the art of healing hands, I sat down to begin reading. The author spoke of intuitive people, sometimes called sensitives, who could read deeply into people in a psychic manner. She also spoke of her own talents of being able to connect with her inner self and the inner selves of her clients. I read nearly thirty pages of a large-size book, when it occurred to me that as I read the author's words, I could hear her voice speaking the words to me.

I questioned myself as to the legitimacy of this. I also looked for a picture of the author in this book to see if I might have imagined a character voice for a shown photograph, but there was none. I thought of other books that I had recently read and considered whether or not I had formulated an author voice for those readings. I was certain that I had not for the last book that I read, and accepted that I could indeed hear the author's voice while reading her work.

I'm Still Here

My best friend, Gwenn, passed away several years ago. We were quite close, and she was my sole mentor in encouraging me on my spiritual path. Through her instruction, I learned to open a channel to the spirit world and gain some form of communication with those on a higher plane.

Gwenn's former husband was quite attentive during her last days on earth, and by her wishes, he disbursed much of her personal belongings to her many girlfriends.

Soon after Gwenn's passing, I was able to see and communicate with her a few times, as I felt I would.

While I seldom remember my dreams, I awoke one morning to find that Gwenn had visited me. "I'm still here," she said. When I awakened, I was so happy and comforted with that finding, as I had missed her dearly.

At the same time, I had a puzzling thought. Why had her husband given away all of her personal belongings if she was still here? Then I realized that she had visited me in my sleep and had let me know that she was still with me on the earth plane, but not in a physical form.

Printed in Fate Magazine

In Flight

My son, a pilot, was flying a few associates to an out-of-town work event. The weather was somewhat turbulent, but while underway, the controls and operation of the plane just did not feel right to him. He struggled with this for some time, not wanting to alarm his passengers.

When he had nearly reached his destination, he flew over some green and yellow balloons that had been tied together and released into the air. His thoughts transferred to my friend who had recently deceased; she was someone for whom he had an attachment and great admiration.

At the memorial service held for her outdoors, her closest friends released green, red and yellow balloons into the air as a tribute to her at the end of the ceremony. He also had released one of those balloons.

As he passed over the balloons in the air, knowing that they were not those released for her, a sudden ease came over him and the airplane. The controls were no longer stiff and the plane had smoothed out. Everything was fine and he was able to land the craft without incident.

It was evident that our friend had an active part in fixing the problem with the plane, and the sign of the balloons was her way of indicating her presence and good deed.

Printed in Fate Magazine

Jack of Spades

My husband and I had been playing a couple of games of cards each night, and on the cut of the deck, a Jack of Spades appeared far too many times to be by chance. This happened several times in one game, and it had been going on for weeks. We knew that it meant something and that it was a message for us, but we weren't able to figure out what it was.

I finally called a psychic friend, Victoria, from Mystic Realms, and asked her what she thought. She didn't have an answer right away, but she called me back a day or two later. She said that her spirit guides told her that a conflict was going to arise, and the Jack was a messenger to tell us to use diplomacy.

The first confrontation was between my husband and his daughter. He thought that she should have used more discretion in dealing with a third party. I agreed with the daughter, which put some friction between my husband and myself. I was anxious to play cards the next evening to see if the Jack of Spades still appeared. It did.

The following night my husband and I attended a party, and our tickets for the event had been pre-paid by check. When we arrived, there were no name tags for us, and we were told that we had not paid. Our check had obviously been lost in the mail, but the lady at the desk was rude and indignant. We were allowed to stay, because we were friends of those in charge, but it put a damper on the evening.

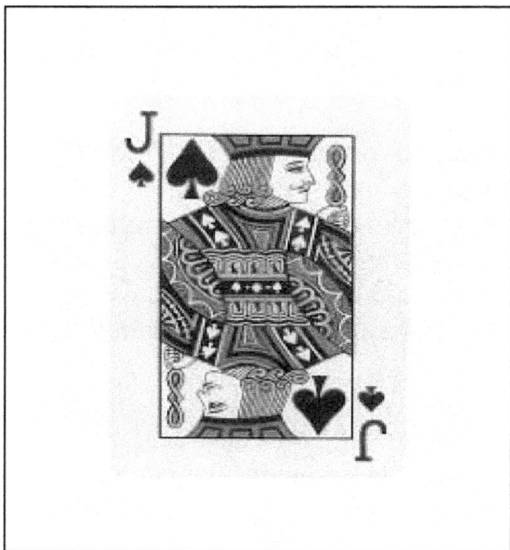

We again played cards, and the Jack of Spades still appeared. "We're not done yet," I said. "It's not gone."

The following night we went to a bowling alley where most of my husband's children and grandchildren bowl on a mixed league. We were surprised to find that no one was there that evening except for one daughter and her husband.

That daughter was very upset, because she learned that all of the others had been invited to one of the granddaughter's college graduation party. My husband was also upset that we were not included in this celebration.

No issues were raised by either slighted party. It was decided to just let it go. Perhaps that was the diplomacy needed.

We played cards again when we returned home that evening. The Jack of Spades did not appear at the cut of the deck. "Maybe that's all of the confrontations for us for a while," I said. "It looks like we're clear."

Joseph

While in an almost slumber state, my guides often show me things in a visual manner that I would not be able to see otherwise.

I was resting on the couch when I saw a vision of a face I knew quite well, but with a lot of facial hair. "My son," I said, as I recognized him.

As I watched, the hair grew and filled in more, and the face began to change into another face I recognized. "Joseph!," I said. Was I being told that my son was once Joseph from the time of Christ?

Just a Glimpse

As I perused the faces of nightly visitors who peered in at me, I saw Jesus looking upon me. He was gone in an instant, but I wondered why he was there.

"Does he know me?" I queried to myself. "Does he feel he needs to check on me occasionally?" I again asked. He has appeared to me clearly two other times and has allowed me to study his features. This time he briefly peered in at me.

Perhaps it is because I was there, long ago, during the time of Jesus. I was told that by a psychic, and this is the passage that she referenced as to when I was present in Jesus' life:

When it was almost time for the Jewish Passover, Jesus went up to Jerusalem. In the temple courts he found men selling cattle, sheep and doves, and others sitting at tables exchanging money. So he made a whip out of cords, and drove all from the temple area, both sheep and cattle; he scattered the coins of the money changers and overturned their tables. To those who sold doves he said, "Get these out of here! How dare you turn my Father's house into a market!"

I entered this article on my Facebook page. This is one response I received to this posting: "Of course He knows you, as he knows everyone else. Jesus wanted you to be aware of this. How wonderful to experience Him!"

Library Ghost

I attended a talk on Henry VIII at a local library with my British friend, Duncan. We met after work and went to dinner prior to going to the library. I had a generous portion of fish and chips, an English favorite, and enough coffee to keep most awake half the night.

However, despite the number of refills to my bottomless cup of coffee and the entertaining lady who spoke at the library, I found myself nodding off during her presentation. The combination of a big meal and the lights turned off for the showing of slides kept me fighting sleep until I gave in.

Duncan nudged me, and I awoke. I still fought sleep, but did again enjoy the storyteller's magnificent presentation. Then Duncan fell asleep and I returned the favor of awakening him.

We were seated in the third row to the left of the center. To my right, a lady in the first row with short, golden hair turned around in her chair and stared at me. She smiled, but I was embarrassed and wondered why she was smiling and staring at me. After all, I was awake now. Why should she stare at me? Our glances exchanged over what seemed like several moments.

Suddenly, she was gone, and I saw the back of the lady with long, dark hair that was sitting in that chair. She had obviously not turned around at all! I then knew that I had clearly seen an entity in the library, just as whole and wholesome looking as you and I.

Lucky Day

My Money Angel often left pennies or small change where I could find it, just to let me know that she was near. I hadn't seen any clues for some time, and I was looking for reassurance that she was still around.

I had been shopping that day and parked the car in the lot. My eyes scanned the ground around me, looking for a penny or two, but none were to be found. I finished shopping, got back into my car, and drove to my next stop.

Again, after parking the car, I perused the ground around me, but found nothing. When I came out of the store and approached my car, there were a couple of attendants collecting shopping carts in the lot. One was directly in back of my car with a string of carts and stopped to pick up something on the ground.

He yelled to the other attendant. "I found a penny. It must be my lucky day!"

Had my Money Angel left it for me? Or, did she feel that the finding of the penny by someone who announced its presence was confirmation enough?

Medicine Woman

From the time I was a young woman, I was extremely interested in medicine. I bought a copy of Taber's Medical Dictionary, and also studied the effects of vitamins, medications, and the interactions between them. I self-diagnosed my own needs as well as those of my friends, and my own family physician respected my opinions when prescribing pharmaceuticals.

I had always felt that I had a close association to medicine from one or more incarnations. I had traveled to England a few years prior in search of previous lives, one of which I learned was as a nurse in an institution.

When my friend, Cassie, returned from visiting with her psychic massage therapist friend in California, she told me that she had learned some interesting insight as to my work in England in a former life.

"What's that?" I inquired.

It was of little surprise to learn of the vision that Cassie's friend, Melissa, saw of me. She said that around the middle of the nineteenth century, I had been a medicine woman in England. The people of the town wanted to run me out, but I fled to France.

I used herbal medicine in my practice, which would have been appropriate for that time. I relocated to an area in France where my work was accepted and I was able to practice there.

Moving Picture

One afternoon when I had a few moments to rest, I laid down on the couch. Thoughts of family members must have been on my mind, and I remember thinking about my late grandfather.

Soon a vision of a young woman, perhaps in her late twenties to very early thirties, appeared. She had long, dark blonde hair and was talking to someone. I so clearly made out her features and watched the movement of her mouth as she spoke.

She was in conversation with an adult, but I could not see that person. She was holding a small male baby in her arms. I did not feel that it was my grandfather, but it may have been him, or one of his brothers. I obviously felt this woman was my grandfather's mother.

I knew nothing about her and have never even seen a picture of her. I doubt that one ever existed in my immediate family. My grandfather had been orphaned by the death of both of his parents at a young age. They died of either diphtheria or scarlet fever. All of the children were taken in by neighbors to be raised with children of their own. My grandfather was raised by a French family.

The clarity in which I saw this woman was intense. The movement of her mouth, and the exactness of her features and facial expressions, made me feel that I should know her well, but I did not. She most definitely bore the resemblance of her offspring, my grandfather.

The vision vanished, but I wanted to see more. I always felt that I let the visions go to quickly, before I had time to study the surroundings or dress of the person. I tried to bring that face in again so that I could watch the movement of her facial expressions while in conversation, but I could not.

The vision changed. I could now see that she was wearing a dress and was walking down the street on a sidewalk. The dress had gathered, short sleeves, a tight bodice, and a moderately full skirt. The dress was cream with black ribbon, or piping, on the bodice of the dress, while the sleeves were a solid cream color. The skirt had a straight-lined design broken by an occasional flower crossing it on the cream-colored background.

It was just like watching a moving picture, seeing her hold a baby, talk to a companion, and then walk down the street. She was my grandfather's mother, and I had the privilege of seeing her.

My Golden Word

For a week and a half I encountered an achy feeling in my left arm. It was such a strange feeling, and I couldn't place my arm anywhere to feel comfortable. The discomfort was so slight, I thought perhaps I had slept on it wrong, or strained it from doing heavy lifting.

I was aware and watchful that this was also a sign of a possible heart attack. I hated the thought of having to go to the hospital, so I waited it out to see if my arm would get better.

I called my doctor's office a couple of times, but could not get an appointment sooner than my previously scheduled time a few days away. I wasn't an emergency case, but I continued to worry.

When I went to bed that evening, I consulted with my late father. He died at the age of sixty with a heart attack because he tried to wait for his doctor to be available. "Is that you, Dad, and am I doing the right thing?" I asked when the white wisp of a spirit visited me.

Normally the white wisps of spirit just float in and around, but this time a spot in the light opened up into the shape of a mouth with a dropped lower jaw. Unfortunately, I could not understand the meaning in the message other than to know that he was present.

The next day I had a talk with God. I said, "Are you going to get me in to get help before something bad happens? Can I trust that I will get help in time?"

When I went to bed, I again got a message. I saw a beautiful script handwriting, written in gold, but I could not make out the words. I watched the flow of writing as the words were written on the page. Immediately after this vision vanished, I saw a dollar bill, but with no denomination.

My interpretation was this. "You have my golden word." And, the green paper currency was presented to substantiate, "In God We Trust."

My Playful Spirit Guide

I closed my eyes for just a moment with the intention of meditating. I had not done that for a very long time. I saw a man before my eyes, dressed rather sharply, and wearing a top hat.

His face was quite fair, and he was very nice looking. He either rose to a standing position, or came out of something like a phone booth or store-front window, and he stood smiling before me.

As I watched him, he appeared to be playful—rather impish I would say. I began to see frame after frame as he moved about.

"Who are you?" I asked. "You're beautiful," I said. He just continued his movements in his playful manner.

In my thoughts I said, "You're my spirit guide, aren't you! Do you have a name?"

I did not get a response, and my mind seemed to play tricks on me. A transfer was made from seeing his beautiful face to a former gentlemen friend Mike's nice looking face.

Was that telling me something? Had he brought playful Mike into my life from a couple of years back? As I was thinking that he did, the frames of watching this playful man faded away.

When I told my friend, Gwenn, of this encounter, she quickly informed me, "He answered you," she said. "His name was Mike. The transfer of his face to Mike's was to tell you his name."

Nancy's Mom's Visit

My dear friend, Nancy, had quite a devastating year. In December she lost her job, and at an age where getting another one was going to be difficult. She was pretty close to being able to get Social Security, but would feel the gap until she was able to collect. I assured her that unemployment would carry her through and she would be all right.

Nancy had two brothers and a mother still alive. One of the brothers lived with the mother and helped to take care of her. In February both that brother and her mom became very ill, and one day Nancy was called upon to come over to assist them. When she arrived, both of them were on the floor and Nancy called '911' to get them both to the hospital. She spent the next week visiting them in different rooms of the same hospital.

While she was making arrangements for her mom to be transferred to a nursing care center, she passed on. The stress was so great that Nancy ended up in the hospital herself.

Unfortunately, without a job, she did not have any health insurance, and it was too soon for Medicare to take over. What a mess she was in. Two months later, her ailing brother died. Such a traumatic set of circumstances for one person to endure.

To help her out of her financial situation, Nancy did get a job at a retail store for a small wage. She was glad to be working, even with such a reduced paycheck, although the hours she spent on her feet were taxing.

The following December while she was at work, a couple came up to her counter pushing a lady in a wheelchair. The lady had white hair and suffered from Alzheimer's just as Nancy's mom did.

The lady looked directly at Nancy. When the couple left, wheeling the lady away, they stopped to shop in an adjacent department. The white-haired lady did not take her eyes off of Nancy. She continued to watch her.

That's when Nancy called me to tell me of some of the strange things that had been happening since her mom passed away. First, she said, "I had a picture of my Mom on my piano in the living room, and every time I would be on the telephone, the picture would fall over," she exclaimed.

"Then," she continued, "when this couple brought that lady to my counter, she looked just like my Mom! Tears just started pouring down my face, and the couple was so nice."

Nancy had not said she looked so much like my Mom, or she reminded me so much of my Mom. She told me she looked just like her Mom.

"Nancy," I said, "did you ever consider that you did see your Mom but in spiritual form?"

"Yes, I did. That's why I'm telling you," she said.

"I'd say your Mom did come to see you," I confirmed.

"Oh," she continued, "I forgot to tell you. It was her birthday!"

Now it was definitely confirmed. When I mentioned this story to my friend, Gwenn, she said, "The message was that 'she is well taken care of.'"

"Oh," I said. "I'll have to tell that to Nancy."

"You just never do get it, do you!" Gwenn laughed as she said that.

I get so wrapped up in the paranormal event that I lose sight of the message.

Negativity in the Air

My husband and I were on our way home from vacation, having spent about ten days in Florida. It was stormy, with rain in the forecast all day.

Traffic was congested, and very slow due to the weather. Negative shadows appeared in the sky on this gloomy day. As we crept along, I saw more negativity in the air. Accidents appeared on the right and on the left sides of the road. The trees actually had dark auras, and I had never noticed trees having auras before at all.

A splat of dark energy covered our entire front windshield as we sat in traffic, waiting for it to move us along. The energy stayed there for a very long time, and I knew that there would be much more trouble on the road ahead. When it removed itself, I was relieved, as I had never seen such negativity out in the open before.

I told my husband about the dark energy that I was seeing, and with the amount of accidents on the road over the next two hours it proved to be true. It took us three hours to drive out of Florida, and as we did, the rain lessened to a mere sprinkle. I was grateful that all of that negativity didn't personally affect us; however, it was something that I saw that I shall not forget.

New Found Spirituality

My son, Doug, had a falling out with his live-in girlfriend, Marjorie. She moved out, they were not on good speaking terms, and it did not appear that they would be working things out. That is when he had a surprise awakening.

He had come over to my house and we sat at the kitchen table having a cup of coffee. His conversation referenced something about his father, and I cautioned him about following in his Dad's footsteps. He remarked, "I have a little of my mother in me, too."

"What do you mean?" I asked.

"Marjorie is regretting what she has done," he said.

"Why do you say that?" I questioned.

"Well, while I was pulling weeds outside in the yard, I kept getting the strongest feelings, with the words, 'Oh my God, what have I done?' directly from Marjorie.

"You just received a telepathic message," I said.
"I've never experienced anything like that before. Now I know what you're talking about."

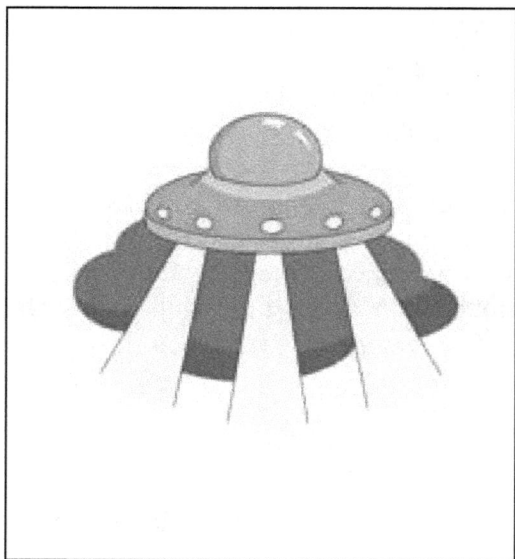

Night Flyer

Night Flyer

At one time I was doing some publicity through a radio station, and one of the people in charge and I exchanged much conversation about paranormal events. Following is a story told by him:

"I saw a UFO. Honestly, I did. It was about 200 to 300 feet above my head. It was triangular and about the size of a football field in length. The place was Shelbyville, Indiana.

I was working for a radio station there, and had stopped by a little drive-in restaurant called Ernie's. They had the best tenderloin sandwiches. The restaurant was owned by Ernie Watkins. He's deceased now.

It was nighttime, and there were six of us that saw it. It was probably going about 500 mph tops. It was awesome, and I'm still reluctant to tell people what I saw. I don't mind if you repeat it, but I'd rather stay anonymous."

Nothing Behind the Eyes

One of my friends questioned a decision she had made in regard to a family member. She went to see a psychic reader for further information. Upon showing the reader a picture of this person, the psychic said: "She has nothing but bad intentions. Look, there is nothing behind the eyes."

Shortly after, another friend of mine had a blood vessel rupture in her eye. She was assisting a business owner in organizing her office. When a long-term employee of the organization was found to be threatening to my friend's success, she worked at getting this person fired.

Her actions were of a vicious nature. While she toiled at this, I saw a great vacancy in the eye with the ruptured blood vessel. There was "nothing behind the eye."

The situation was skillfully corrected by the business owner, and the long-term employee did not lose her job. My friend's eye then returned to its normal state.

Notice of Change

I hadn't met with Cassie socially for a very long time. We had planned to get together over the summer when she was not teaching school, but her vacation to Mexico and other things seemed to postpone our plans to the Fall season.

When we finally got together, she wanted to tell me of her excitement of buying a condo for herself. "It all happened so smoothly, I just knew it was meant to be," she said.

We met for dinner one evening, and she told me her story. She had already gotten undressed and was in her pajamas when the telephone rang. It was her real estate agent who called to say that she had a condo she wanted her to see.

"I'm already in my pajamas," Cassie said.

"Well don't change. I'll put mine on," the agent said. And, they went to the lady's home who had the condo for sale. The lady received them, also in her pajamas. Cassie knew in an instant this was the condo unit for her and made an offer.

The timing was perfect. She was a teacher, and would be closing just in time to be able to move during the Easter break at school. She was very excited about her new home.

I then told her my story of when I was about to purchase another home, and that I kept finding change everywhere I went. It was to such an extreme that I began to know that I would find small amounts of money, and that they were to be found by me.

The message was that a change was going to take place in my life.

"Oh," Cassie said, "I've been finding a lot of change myself. It's very unusual for me, too. I hadn't thought about it actually meaning a "change."

Oh, So Beautiful!

I've been blessed with the ability to see many entities of the spirit world, and I recently decided to reflect on the many guides I've actually seen.

After having attended a psychic class where I was told about one of my guides and her physical appearance, Greta appeared to me in God's white circle of light. That was the first time that I actually saw a guide or a white circle of light.

"She's quite old, and not very spiritual," I was told. "She wants to be called Greta, and she comes with a rolling pin in her hand. She is here to see that you take good care of yourself."

I've also been told about Ralph, another guide, by a channeler. She told me that he had red hair and was jolly, but he has never appeared to me in the mind's eye. However, one day on a return trip from New Orleans, I met a man on the plane who dressed as I had pictured Ralph, was friendly, and had red hair.

Then one evening, after seeing a movie on television, I admired a beautiful young actress with attractive dark eyes and dark hair. I didn't know her name, but I was taken with her beauty.

111

Soon after, a beautiful angel appeared in my psychic vision after retiring for the night. She also had gorgeous dark eyes and lovely dark hair, and allowed me to study her face for some time. She blinked her eyes, just as we do, and turned her head slightly away and then back to look at me.

I was so drawn to the actress' beauty that I can't help but think that my angel wanted me to appreciate her beauty as well. I certainly did, as she was oh, so beautiful!

On My Birthday

I had often heard of others remarking that something noteworthy happened in their lives to remind them of loved ones passed on, either on that person's birthday or the date of their death. They felt that there was a presence around them or that a message had been given by something that happened.

On my recent birthday, I had traveled out of town and had retired for the night after a lovely evening of fine dining and great music. I had worn a red dress and shoes, and matching red lipstick for the outfit.

The coffee I drank during the evening kept me from going right to sleep, and I welcomed the encounters from visiting spirits as I lie awake. A white light would come into view, and I would wait for a manifestation to appear. Sometimes I would only see light forms, but this evening I saw several faces that I did not know.

When I nearly fell asleep, a bright light flashed before my eyes with a notable spark, and a vision of my late mother and her sister appeared. It was nice to see them together, and good to see my mother finally at peace. I welcomed their visit openly.

The vision faded, and I again tried to sleep. Another bright flash of light and a spark awakened me, and my mother again appeared. This time she was all dressed up, her hair was nicely done, and she wore a bright red lipstick. I must have reminded her of her life at my age, and she was acknowledging how I looked that evening.

Paranormal and the Bible Belt

Hopefully no one will take offense to this cute true story. I was traveling through some of the Bible Belt states, and somewhere in Kentucky I stopped at a college bookstore to donate a couple of my books.

A young lady was at the cash register where I inquired if they sold any other books than textbooks. "Why yes," she said. "Students always like to read other material."

I explained that I had books of a topic that was not too popular in that area; namely, I had books of a paranormal nature, and asked her what she thought.

She suggested that many of the Unity churches would be interested in my material, and I countered that I had thought about that.

I wish I could write in that delightful southern accent to continue this story. However, she said in her elongated accent, "This is the B-i-b-l-e Belt. And e-v-e-r-y-o-n-e will tell you that t-h-e-y are not interested, but t-h-e-y want to k-n-o-w!"

She was so taken with one of the books that I held in my hand, that I said to her, "Why don't you just have this book! I'd love to give it to you."

Passing

She was such a good pal, always welcoming me when I came home. Her soft little purr and brush against my leg let me know just how much she cared. When her age became such that her time was near, she followed me around the house as she did when she was a kitten. I sensed her trying to let me know that she would not be here long.

Her appetite grew slight and her color drabbed, yet her affections stayed the same. As I worked outside in the yard, she took her last walk through, stopping to rest at points where she never stopped before. She looked around as if to take in the last sight of her surroundings. She seemed complacent with this excursion.

The following morning she drank water, but her appetite was absent. Her eyes sank deeper and she slept near me as I moved about the house. I knew her time was near. I made arrangements with the veterinarian for late afternoon.

It was a very personal experience between us, my cat and me. When once she meowed noisily all the way to the veterinarian's office, she now purred in her almost comatose state. She was comforted to know that I was with her and that she would soon get help.

117

I left her in the doctor's hands, the chore difficult enough to do. Within thirty minutes after leaving her, she let me know that she had passed and was still around me. A strong vibrational sound in my ear announced her presence and I knew that it was her.

For the following week she meowed in the early morning hours as I awakened, and brushed by my legs throughout the day to let me know that she was there.

I was glad that she was around, as I missed her, but I gave her permission to leave, and to go into the light and go home. I knew it would be a more beautiful place for her to be.

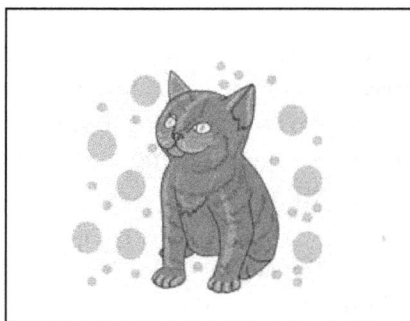

Photo Shots

I wish I knew who visits me, either by the vibration I hear and feel in an ear, or the visual experiences I have when resting before sleep. I know someone is there, and even though I query, few show their face or let me know who they are when I ask. I'm sure that I have more than a few guides that help me, but it would be so nice to know who brings me information.

The other evening, before my sound sleep, someone brought me several photo shots of dear family members, now deceased. I saw a picture of my mother as a young woman, before an age that I would have known her. Then, one followed of her mother, my grandmother, also at an age that I would not have ever known; her sister, my aunt, and then another aunt from my father's side.

Were they all together now? Is that what the guide was trying to show me? When I asked to know who was present to bring me information, was that my answer? Were all of these loved ones around to assist me at one time or another?

Pixie

I was working with some clip art on my computer to use on a craft project. I found a selection of clear objects that I wanted to use: a pencil, a tape dispenser and a ruler. I copied each to a separate word file. When I opened up the first file, a pixie was sitting on the end of the pencil.

"Now where did that come from?" I wondered. "I'll have to get that off of there." I then brought up the file in an artwork program so that I could erase the pixie from the pencil. When I opened the file, the pixie was gone. Amazed with this, I went back to my original word file. The pixie wasn't there either.

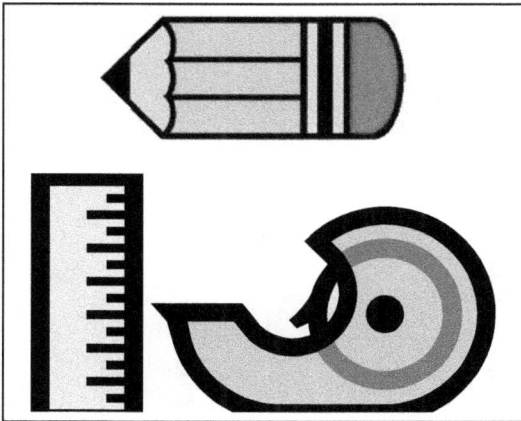

I was perplexed by this for the next few days. Then I remembered that a little pixie had visited me a couple of times earlier in the year in my psychic eye's vision.

Sometime later, she again presented herself to me on my computer screen. She was in a seated position, head resting on her hand, and propped up on one elbow. She was tapping the fingers of one hand as if to say, "I'm waiting . . ."

She was still trying to deliver her message that my answers would be found in nature, or all things natural, and didn't understand why I didn't get it.

Powerful People

I related a phenomenal incident to an intuitive psychic from California who was visiting my friend, Cassie. I told her how my Tarot card reader and friend had given me names of psychic persons and store owners to contact for the publisher of a psychic newspaper that printed articles that I wrote.

One of the names was of her mother, although they did not share a good relationship.

As I typed up the list of names, I soon felt that I was being contacted by my friend's mother. I knew that it was she, but only in my subconscious mind. I therefore mentally noted the attempt of contact and went on about my work. A little later in the day, she tried to contact me once more. Again, I mentally noted the attempt and continued whatever I was doing.

When I went to bed that evening, the mother was there again. This time I greeted her by name and explained that I knew she had been trying to reach me all day. She responded by showing me a group of white lighters, but said nothing. When the floor tilted and the wall began to open in my vision, I spoke to her. I said, "What is going on? I don't understand what is happening."

This time she verbally responded and I heard the voice of my friend's mother. I asked Cassie's psychic friend how she could possibly speak to me and what did she want? I was told that she had enough power to be able to project herself there for a limited time, and that she wanted to know who that powerful person was that was associating with her daughter!

Propeller

Often times I get a feeling inside when meeting someone. Most of the time it is because the person is so snarled inside and gives off such a strong sense of pain or confusion. Other times I pick up if someone is bi-polar, has had some misfortunate event happen in their lives, or is carrying some burden that is detectable to me.

I had a contractor working at my house doing a small addition on my home. Because he was there daily over a few months' time, I got to know him well, and we even talked about his wife. His wife became curious about my gift of reading people and asked what I saw in her husband.

I explained, "His spirit appeared to me as a propeller. The motor that drives the propeller runs intermittently. Energy is built up to turn the blades a full turn or cycle, then winds down to a few second stall. It then revs up again, and the process repeats itself," I told her.

"Abrupt starts and stops," she said.

"Yes, but always moving forward."

She laughed, but I could tell that she fully understood the synchronicity of the message and how it related to her husband.

Red Eyes

My eyesight had always been pretty good with near 20/20 vision. As I've aged, however, I've experienced dryness of the eyes, and my doctor has prescribed stronger eye drops every year after my exam. However, finding the eye drops unpleasant to use, I soon stopped using them each time.

Finding a dark spot within the white of one of my eyes, I made an appointment to have my eyes checked. The doctor said that my eye was inflamed, and he prescribed even heavier gel eye drops, telling me to use them at night before going to bed and more often if I wanted to. This time I tried to abide.

Still, redness would appear at the bottom of the eyes, and I continued to forget to use the drops before going to bed. Sometimes I used them in the morning, but I knew that I probably needed them morning and night.

It was late in the evening when I decided I was tired enough to sleep. I got myself ready for bed, and crawled in, forgetting the eye drops. Soon my mind's eye began its nightly work of providing images, and often of people I do not know.

I normally see a white cast background, knowing that the information is directly from God. This time the entire backdrop was a vibrant red. I didn't think this was a good sign, so I began to recite the words I knew to ask for protection in God's white light.

The red persisted, and then I knew. I was being reminded that I had forgotten to use the eye drops and would have red eyes in the morning if I didn't use them.

Red Hearts

My dear and lasting girlfriend of many years passed away after a very long battle with cancer. During the last year of her life, I found a male companion who later became my husband. She felt somewhat hurt, feeling that I would be giving her less attention.

After her passing, she visited me a few times. On one of her visits, she blessed me with several thin outlines of red hearts, letting me know that she approved of our marital union and no longer felt slighted.

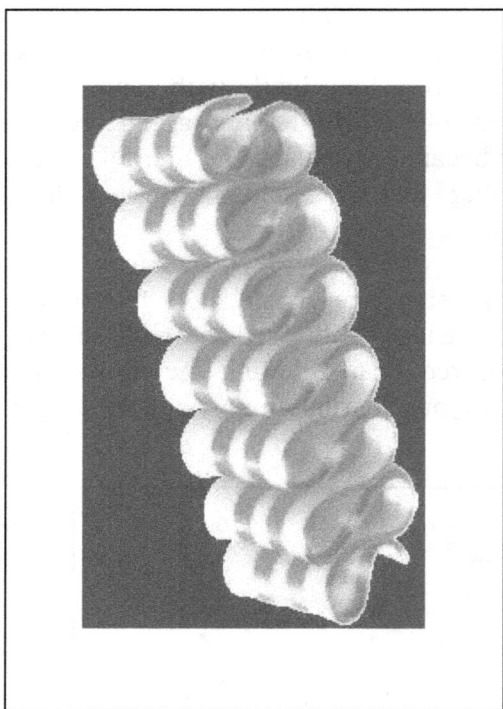

Ribbon Candy

Ribbon Candy

At my Aunt Addie's funeral, I had the opportunity to see out-of-state relatives that I hadn't seen in years. I also met my cousin's daughter, Lorraine, for the first time. She was a delightful, warm and friendly young woman, and we later established an ongoing connection through the Internet.

Lorraine learned of my strange-but-true symbolic readings of people and asked me if I had ever received a vision of her dad. I said no, but the next day I saw a mental picture and sent an e-mail back with the words "Ribbon Candy." I then passed the information on to her dad as follows:

"Your daughter, Lorraine, asked if I had seen a vision of you. I replied that I had not, but a delayed vision appeared and I saw 'ribbon candy' in my mind's eye."

My interpretation: "A very sweet and colorful person whose life has had multiple paths and interests, and moderate-to-extraordinary ups and downs." His response was this:

"Believe me, there was no offense. I thought the vision quite interesting and much on the mark."

Sharing Space
with a Spirit

A whoosh of air
briskly encircles your body
within a cool nanosecond.
What was it?

Then you realize
that you have just
brushed your way
through an angelic spirit.

"Pardon me!"
I say to the spirit world.
"I am so sorry to have
stepped into your space."

Spirit

My closest friend had passed on, and a memorial was held for her in my backyard one beautiful fall day, just as she had requested.

I was visited by her in my meditative state a few times right after her death, but then she did not come.

I did not hear from her for some time, so one night as I began to enter my meditative state, I asked for her. She did not come. I asked for her again, but there was still no response. Then I asked for her a third time, and she arrived, in spirit form.

I sensed that she was exuberant with her new existence and surroundings, and I was happy for her. I could also hear her voice in her usual excitable chatter, but nothing was audible to me.

We exchanged feelings of love. She gave me a special hug of energy, and then her spiritual being vanished into the heavens.

Spiritual Kisses

My dearest friend, Gwenn, passed away much too young for her vibrant spirit. She was just 62. She is the one who mentored me on my psychic path, even though she was unable to see the visions herself. She had a sense of intuition that was quite keen, and the intellect to go along with it.

After her sad departure, she visited me, as I knew she would. The first time she let me know that she was very angry at her friends for discouraging an out-of-town friend, Kaye, from visiting her before her death.

Gwenn visited many times, and let me know that she was aware of how much I missed her. Although I had seen her a few times in my mind's eye, this time I could not. However, I clearly felt her presence. She embraced me warmly, and offered her spiritual kisses to let me know that I was also loved.

St. Germain's Appearance

For the past several years, I have seen a vision in the mind's eye of a bluish purple circle with ragged edges and yellow around the outside. I knew it was a spirit, and misnamed it St. Michael. The same vision appeared to me countless times, and finally the owner of a psychic store convinced me that what I was seeing was the Violet Flame, brought by St. Germain.

My confusion stemmed from the fact that when I researched the Violet Flame on the Internet, it was shown to be violet with a yellow center. What I saw had the yellow on the outside of the violet circle. After some time I accepted that it must be the Violet Flame.

Although I seem to have great difficulty recalling the name St. Germain when his bluish purple light appears, I have come to address him as such. His visits have become more frequent, and because I still question the difference in the position of the violet and yellow light, he kindly changes the yellow to the center to reassure me, and then reverts to his usual stance.

To add to my uncertainty, I often see just a yellow circle, or glow, enter my mind's eye. Some research indicated that the yellow light is from St.

Michael. Sometimes he gives my page a yellow cast when I'm reading a spiritual book.

I later learned that St. Germain and St. Michael often work together.

On two recent occasions, a male figure, having light hair and a slightly rugged appearance showed up just prior to my vision of the Violet Flame. "That must be St. Germain," I presumed. However, a few nights later, a dark-haired figure with softer features appeared right in the center of the Violet Flame.

Now I am certain that St. Germain definitely showed himself there so that I would not be confused as to his identity. The man with the light hair was St. Michael.

The Following

Upon meeting my friend, Katie, I could feel the anguish and turmoil within her, so much so that it was uncomfortable for me to be around her. One day, as we were seated near one another at a luncheon, we struck up a conversation that centered around the subject of spiritual entities.

I told her about the books that I write, and she was then comfortable in talking to me about her tribulations in life and the spirits she felt around her.

She also asked me if I knew a good tarot card reader. I made arrangements to take her to one I'm fond of, and who helped her immensely with the consternation that she felt inside.

Although she is still troubled, I no longer feel the tension within her. Much of her pain has been healed.

She often speaks of seeing quick flashes of a being in her home that she feels is her father. Other times, she sees a gray shadow, and also feels her father's presence. Sometimes a communication from him takes place that puts words in her head.

Quite recently, she was doing some quick shopping, and someone approached her and said, "There's someone following you, you know."

There was no one else around. "Oh, it's probably my father," she responded, and hurried on her way.

She made her next stop at a grocery store. She was picking out goods from the shelves and putting them in her cart, when she noticed a man approaching her in a wheelchair. He said, "You know there is someone following you."

Again, she said, "Oh yes, that's probably my father." The conversation with the man continued, and Katie was unable to get away from him.

As she continued to shop, the man followed her and kept talking. He was beginning to scare her. She finally said, "I'm really loving this conversation, but I really must go." She then hurriedly checked out and left the store.

The man followed her out into the parking lot and approached her car before she could get away. She quickly picked up her cell phone and pretended to talk with someone as she waved good bye and sped away.

"Twice in the same day," she exclaimed, "someone I didn't even know told me that I was being followed. I wish I wasn't in such a hurry. Perhaps I could have learned more."

Sometimes we miss opportunities that are presented to us because of our preoccupation or the pressure of completing a task. It probably is, but wouldn't she be surprised to find that it isn't her father following her at all?

The Hanging

I receive much of my psychic information through visual imagery. I had been enjoying little bits of information that I found to be useful, until one evening I saw a young black girl hung by her wrists, just outside a window near a back door of my home. The vision saddened me, and I've been searching for reasons why she was hung ever since. My home is situated on a parcel in an area that is known to have been an Indian burial ground.

That vision stuck with me and made my heart ache for many days . Soon after, my son came over and went outside through the back door. I could see that he suddenly lost equilibrium as he passed through the doorway, right next to the window where the hanging took place.

Next, I passed through that same doorway and also momentarily lost equilibrium. That never happened before seeing the vision, but now I find that the energy from the hanging must still be there.

The Inner Demon

I met a man in a social setting where there was dancing and alcoholic beverages. Most people in that atmosphere were drinking socially and having a good time, while this man was friendly and quite inebriated. While I tried to appreciate his offer of friendship, I found it difficult to overlook his drunken condition.

The next day I kept hearing a voice. It was the voice of the drunken man's inner demon. When I stopped to listen, I could hear this demon posing as a friendly advisor. It would be difficult to feel that he was harmful and not a friend. I could also see him in my mind's eye. He was a small brown creature and lived in a pouch of the man's belly, much like a kangaroo holds its young. He had two sets of big floppy ears, somewhat like elephant ears.

I knew that the man would think the voice was his own thinking, or his own conscience guiding him. I wish that I could see him again so that I could tell him about his inner self. I would tell him to spend more time with God. He needed to exorcise this demon and tell him to go away. I would explain that at some point he allowed this demon in, and that he didn't have to let him stay. He must be strong and force him to leave in order to have a better life.

The Madam

One of the ladies of our sewing club, a group of girls who have met for many years, appeared to have the attributes of a Madam. She was a large, attractive woman, with delicate and poised hands and beautiful nails.

She would say, "Now girls," as if she was directing her harem. We had nicknames for some of the more notable girls in the club, and we called Celia "The Madam," meaning a woman who runs a brothel.

One day Celia fell and broke her leg. She was in the ambulance and on her way to the hospital when she had a series of memorable events run through her mind. She remembered them clearly and wrote them down for me.

On the way to the hospital, she was in a state of unconsciousness. Among the many things that she reported, was being in a house which had a bar and floor made of marble. She recalls all sorts of people laying around and some of them having sexual activity.

She told me, "The bar reminded me of back in Jesus' time with all of the angels. Images of flowers and angels appeared on the sides of the bar. There was a swimming pool behind the bar that was

147

filled with a substance like porcelain. After the people went into the pool, they were turned into statues. A man jumped into the pool and came out as a flying angel."

She was quite perplexed as to what all of this meant. A few of the girls in the club who learned of this information certainly wondered if she was, indeed, at some point in her past lives, a Madam of a brothel.

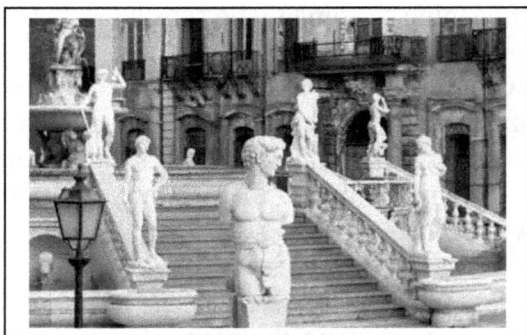

Palermo, Piazza Pretoria
Lachris77

The Music of Angels

I had retired for the evening, and my thoughts wandered as I waited for sleep to come. As my mind drifted from one thing to another, I suddenly realized that I heard beautiful music. It was music that I had never heard the likes of before. Then I realized that it was coming from angels. It had no rhythm, beat, or melody, just beautiful harmony.

I recalled reading about the music of angels, and found them listed in a book as joyous singers. One type is called Cherubim, and their purpose is to assist with insomnia. The other is Seraphim, that help you remember your dreams.

While I rarely have trouble sleeping, I also rarely remember my dreams. Perhaps the Seraphim thought I should recall a dream for a message that would be given me. Unfortunately, I didn't remember any dream the next morning.

On another evening that I had trouble falling asleep, I again heard the music of angels, but not as clearly as I had heard before.

The Pearl is Within the Lotus

One evening I was taking a walk with a gal who was visiting from California. We each talked a little about our backgrounds, and finding some similarities to which we could both relate, began exchanging stories. Her spiritual story is one I am repeating here.

She had a boyfriend in California, but the relationship was not going well. An acquaintance offered her an opportunity to take a job working in Tibet, and she elected to go. She figured that her relationship was not going that well anyway, and she could use a change. The experience of going there to work and to learn of the people and their culture was also quite intriguing.

She spent enough time in Tibet to appreciate the beliefs and behaviors of the Tibetan people, but missed her friends and family. At holiday time, she booked a flight to come home to be with her family, and also her estranged boyfriend.

He had missed her, and she him, and he asked her to marry him. She was uncertain, but with the input from her friends decided that it was the right thing to do.

When she went back to Tibet, she told her friends there of her plans, and they gleefully helped her pick out a dress for her wedding. She wanted a wedding that would tie her newly found surroundings to her future life back home.

Her Tibetan friends helped her shop, but each dress that she tried on did not fit well in one place or another from the sizes that were in stock. It was decided that a dress would be special ordered, and that it could be shipped to her home in the United States.

Still worrying about her decision to marry, she confided in a girlfriend in Tibet. "Ah, she said. You worry, but the pearl is within the lotus." She was telling her that the answer and her feelings were within herself. No one else could answer for her.

Julien Groadin

When she arrived home, she found a boxed package containing her wedding dress. Upon opening it, she tried it on and it fit beautifully.

Satisfied, she took the dress off and placed it on a hanger, noticing the label inside the dress. It said, "The Pearl is Within the Lotus," and she knew then that she had been given a sign and had made the right choice.

The Rising

A gentle, good-hearted man named Norman was raised in a religious family. Later in life, he became an atheist, and had no more to do with the church. He married, had a family and a good life.

When he was struck with cancer, his wife stood by and cared for him well. In his final stages in the hospital, in hospice, he faded in and out of consciousness. When awake, he spoke to unseen people above him, giving his acknowledgement. Both his wife and his nurse were witness to this.

His wife pleaded with him to make peace with God. "You're a sinner," she said. "Ask God to forgive you, and he will." Her pleas were met with disdain.

For three days before his death, he said, "I'm rising. I'm rising." But his life lingered on. The nurse finally told his wife, "You're going to have to let him go. There are people here waiting to take him."

"I'm not ready to let go," she said. Finally, she consented, and he passed peacefully, his soul finally rising to the heavens.

The Wizard Speaks

There was a point in my life that I was called upon to solidify my relationship with my son. It had to do with love, trust, and money. At that time, he was at a point of losing his house to creditors due to business losses. I didn't feel I was in a position to save him, if I needed to do so, but would do whatever I could.

During this ordeal, Doug found two buyers for his home that would have saved his credit, but for some unknown reasons, his bankruptcy lawyer intervened, and he was unable to complete the sale in each instance. He may not have been advised correctly; however, he was paying for this service and felt it was in his best interest not to complete either sale.

In the meantime, the home was taken from him and he had a six-month redemption period in order to reclaim his rights to the home. Six months passed, and a new mortgage could not be obtained due to liens and levies on the title which had to be cleared.

While eviction papers were coming at him regularly, he satisfied all liens on the property. He again tried to repurchase his own home from the mortgage company who bought it, since it no longer belonged to him.   Again, a title search showed the same liens and levies had not been removed.

"Did Doug close on his house yet?" asked Gwenn, who had just returned from vacation.

"No," I said. "The title is still not clear."

"He's so close, but still not there," she exclaimed. Knowing that I would come to the table in this one, she said—from the internal wisdom of Gwenn— there is something that has to happen before he can close on that mortgage. It's something small, but it has to happen before he will be able to close. I want to say it has to do with Doug or you, or maybe even Marjorie, his live-in girlfriend. Whatever it is, it is very small. The Wizard has spoken!" she said, and we both laughed.

I knew that this information was coming to her magically, as it always did, and she was relaying the message.

We talked more, and something I said sparked the comment "It's not with Marjorie, it has something to do with either you or Doug or you and Doug together. Marjorie isn't part of it."

I waited for more information, and we laughed again about the karmic information, or lack of. "I don't' have the answer," she continued. "I just have the information to give you direction."

Pichayasri

Soothsayers never do give explicit information—just enough for you to try to figure it out yourself, I thought.

"You can always pray to St. Anthony," she said.

"Okay, I said. I'll pray to him."

Before praying, and while writing, I believed that the answer had been given to me. I believed I was being told to get the sideline legal documentation ready between Doug and myself so that we would both be protected with a money transfer for his ownership of the home should I need to assist. Perhaps then he would be able to consummate a successful mortgage closing.

I expressed my feelings to Gwenn. "No, she said, the legality things are important, but I feel it is a karmic debt or requirement that has to be made. I still say it is small, like an apology, a lesson, or the closing down of something. You did pray to St. Anthony, didn't you?"

"Yes," I said. "I prayed to him even after I thought I had the answer."

"Good. The answer will come."

The answer was that Doug needed to know that I would be there to support him in time of need, both emotionally and financially, if need be. When I let him know that I would be there for him, our relationship became quite solid, and has remained as such, many years hence.

There They Were

For some time I had been asking to see an angel. I had read a book about angels, and found that they rarely were seen by humans. It was also reported that some angels are very large and much taller than we are. Still, I had had so many spiritual encounters, I desired to see an angel.

One evening, while attending a meeting at a bookstore, I saw the golden light of a reflection of an angel on the carpeting before me. It was noted and appreciated, but I still did not feel that I had actually seen an angel.

And sometimes when I read, I find that there is a golden cast of light upon the words. I also note that this is from some angelic spirit around me, and I am comforted. Still, I had not actually seen an angel.

Then one night, as I lay down to sleep, my mind was open and ready to receive spiritual interaction. First, I saw vibrant blocks of color, which puzzled me. Then, the blocks moved away, and I saw many angels, both male and female.

They had wings, widespread, gliding through the air and were peering at me through the small window of my mind's eye. There they were. Angels, before my very eyes, in a way that only I could see.

161

Tinker Bell

I was experiencing visual portrayals of a sweet little fairy in my mind's eye after I went to bed at night. She had come to me a few times, but I didn't understand why she was there. I called her Tinker Bell.

I had been asking the universe what I needed to do to solve a particular problem. This time when she appeared, she stated telepathically, "I'm surprised that no one has told you;" but no further information was given.

Later, I found her to appear on my computer screen sitting on top of some artwork I was trying to use for a craft project. Still puzzled by her appearances and the message I was to understand, she then appeared on a license plate of a car that passed me on my way home one evening. The letters were: TNKRBEL.

It was many months before I realized what this earthly entity was trying to convey. I had been doctoring and using much medication but not getting well. She was trying to tell me that I should get back to basics and be cured by nature.

To See an Angel

Ever since I began my spiritual journey, I've been presented with many experiences. It seems that the spirit world wants me to encounter enough events to understand the enormity of what is beyond our current world. I've questioned much and received many answers.

Despite the many spiritual encounters that I've had, I still asked to see an angel. I wanted to have that experience. I discounted the fact that I have seen my guardian angel clearly in my mind's eye. And, I dismissed the fact that I was protected in a car accident by the unseen angel that swept me up in its wings.

Then I read a book that said that very few people have actually seen an angel, so I considered that my request was too much to ask. One evening, as I was attending a group meeting and all were sitting in chairs formed in a circle, I was soon to be appeased with another type of viewing.

As I stared at the carpeting in the middle of the ring of people, I saw four gold bars light up on the floor. That got my attention, and as I waited, I could faintly see the gold cast of an angel with large wings upon the floor.

Even though angels rarely show themselves in full projection, I believe this was an attempt to satisfy my request.

True Picture

This is a story told to me by one of my neighbors.

"My husband and I were on vacation and having a great time. We made friends with a couple across the table from us one night when we were having dinner. They were quite sociable, and before the evening was over, we took pictures of them in memory of our wonderful time.

After we got back home and I had the pictures developed, the picture of the nice couple was not so wonderful. They had the most peculiar look about them that it made me terribly uncomfortable.

They looked evil, and I got a feeling I had not gotten from being with them. It disturbed me so badly that I tore the picture up and threw it out. The photograph had shown me something about them we did not learn in person."

Two, Two

Katie, my clairvoyant friend, received many spiritual messages during the last month of her mom's life. Her mom had a serious surgery, which had complications, and she went into a coma. She was still in the hospital when she died.

A message kept waking Katie up with the presentation of the numerals "two, two; two, two," over and over again. She couldn't figure out what that meant, and conferred with her siblings to see if they could shed any light on the matter.

No one could, but after her mom passed away, one of the sisters called her. "Now I know what the 'two, two' meant," she said.

"What's that?" Katie inquired.

"Mom was in the hospital for twenty-two days, and someone was trying to tell you how long she would have to linger in that coma state."

Verily, Verily

Many read verses in the bible and gain words of insight and wisdom about living a good life and doing what is right. Following the divine word of God gives much comfort and a feeling of belonging to the group of worshipers.

While I was not raised with any religion, I seem to be gifted with a closeness to God with clairvoyance and clairaudience.

When I was reading a church paper, several verses were being quoted, and when reading one in particular, I could hear Jesus' voice. "Verily, verily, I say unto you, He that believeth in Me hath everlasting life."

When I read others, the voice went away.

Other readings have provided similar results of the writer's voice being heard by me. One is a book of hands-on healing, and another is a natural health newsletter to which I subscribed. When the author actually writes the words, I hear them said by the writer. When an editor has made revisions, I find that the voice disappears.

Then, one day while reading "The Daily Word," I could hear Mother Mary's voice as I read the following words:

"My heart is filled with promise, peace, and love."

At the bottom of the page was written:

Mary treasured all these words and pondered them in her heart. – Luke 2:19.

Voices of Angels

I see visual imagery all of the time, but nobody talks to me. At least it is quite rare if they do. I'm expected to interpret the symbolic images that I see in order to get the message. I've often complained to the spirit world that I want to hear words.

Then one day while looking for information on the Internet, I came across an article that explained how to clear your ear chakras so that you can hear your angels. So, when I went to bed, in my mind I fervently mentally cleaned and scrubbed my ears as directed.

I've known that I've had a "Money Angel" all of my life, as she has always made sure that I had just enough money. Sometimes a check would come in the mail, just when it was needed, or I would find small change on the ground, generally pennies, just to let me know that she was there. I've learned to count on her presence.

The first night an angel spoke to me, it was my "Money Angel," a female voice, who clearly said, "Here's a little money for you." I was in awe, but so pleased that she actually talked to me,

No one spoke to me again. So, I repeated the exercise of clearing the ear chakras. I had just learned that the deep blue violet light that I so often see is actually the Violet Flame brought by St. Germain. When I completed the second cleansing, the next voice I heard was male, and he said, "You have nothing to fear."

I asked a psychic friend if she thought that was St. Germain himself. She hesitated as if to wait for a guide to answer, and said "No, I don't think so, but I feel it was one of his helpers." I think it was St. Germain.

Printed in Fate Magazine

Wake Up Dead

It was winter, and an ice storm had come through and knocked out power in several of the surrounding cities. My city, fortunately, was not harmed. I found small tree branches that had fallen across my driveway, but relatively little damage from the severely high winds.

My friend, Gwenn, however, was in a city that had been hit hard, and she was without power for four days. I, personally, would not have survived well with no heat. Being without electricity and all of our modern conveniences, including light, would have been most disturbing, but my body has always demanded a good supply of heat. Using the strength and determination that she had, Gwenn stayed huddled in her house with her two cats and survived.

Among the other inconveniences of having everything in her refrigerator defrost, she was concerned about the smell of what might be a freon leak. That concerned her more than the loss of food, and as soon as her power went on late one evening, she opened up the doors to let fresh air flow through her home. The refrigerator went back on and appeared to be operating normally, but her comment was that the reason she did that was "so she did not wake up dead the next morning."

Her chatter continued without missing a beat, when I stopped her and repeated, "So you don't wake up dead? Do you realize what you just said?" and I laughed at her.

"Well, it's true, isn't it?" implying that even when you die, your soul lives on. You just merely find yourself dead and not a living being on this earth. "You know what I mean."

When in Doubt

When it comes to religion, I have always been a doubter. As a child, I was afraid not to claim that I believed in God, for all of my friends said that they did. As I grew older, I was given many reasons to believe, and by some standards, proof, that God did indeed exist.

Because of my spiritual inclination, I have received countless variations of visual proof that there is a spiritual world, and that spirits, angels and entities do exist. Still, I had doubt.

I believed in this super power God, but then I wondered if Jesus actually did exist. Then, on two separate occasions, Jesus appeared to me in my very vivid internal eye. Each time, he rose up into view and allowed me to study him.

Still, I questioned. I didn't buy in to the many stories surrounding Jesus' life, and presumed that there were many translations by different writers over time who recorded such stories. Which ones would be right?

Or should I believe that Jesus was just a great prophet, and not the son of God as some religions teach. Should I believe in the many characters involved in Jesus' life and believe in their existence as well?

Then one evening I attended a musical event at a church gathering. These questions were still in my head as the music played. I sat several rows back in the audience when the visions began to appear.

My messenger used the backs of the heads of the people sitting in the rows in front of me. There was a display of many of the people in Jesus' life at the time that he was on earth.

Why?, Why?, Why?

Gwenn was going to be driving to Indiana to visit a girlfriend, Kaye, and her husband for a few days over the holiday break. They had tentatively arranged for her to arrive on Sunday and return home on Tuesday.

On Saturday, Gwenn went out to pick up a few things from the store. While driving, she noted a license plate that contained the letters "YYY." She recognized this as a message, but she didn't know what it meant. When she returned home, there were three phone messages left on her answering machine from her friend in Indiana.

First message: Don't bother driving here; we're coming to Michigan. I'll call you later. Second message: Cancel that. My husband's kids have changed their plans and we're not coming now. It's a beautiful day; why don't you come today? Third message: I don't know if we're coming there or you're coming here. We're going out now. I'll call you later.

Ellen received a call from Gwenn saying, "I got the 'YYY' message, but I didn't know what it meant until I got home! Now I'm waiting to find out what I'm supposed to do."

Worker of Light

When I go to bed at night, I ask for God's white light of protection before going into a meditative state. I also often ask, "Is anyone there?" as many times I am visited by several people that I do not even know.

These people peer over me as I lie there in bed. Most are middle age and older, but occasionally there is an infant in my view. I always wondered who they are and why they came to me.

One evening, Melissa and Cassie came to meet me for dinner. Melissa, who had a massage and intuitive healing business, was visiting from California. In discussion, I asked her about these visitors that I had.

"Oh," she said, "You must wake up very tired in the morning." I replied that I did not and asked her why she said that.

"You are a worker of light. They are there to draw upon your energy so that they can stay on the earth plane. Your guides are also there with you to protect you. They will see that too much energy is not taken from you."

Would You Like to Join Us?

My husband and I were vacationing in Florida, and stayed in a motel with a very nice swimming pool. We had just returned to our room after lunch, and were discussing changing into our swim suits.

I looked toward the window, with curtains still drawn, and saw a transparent lady against the wall in the upper left corner of the room.

"There's a lady present with us," I said to my husband. "She's in the upper left corner of the room. I wonder what she is doing here."

"Really," he said. "I've heard you talk about these people, but I've never been with you when you've seen one."

Now I spoke to the lady. She looked elderly and pleasant. I told her that we were going to go swimming and that she was welcome to join us in the pool area.

Of course, she didn't answer, and if she followed us into the bright sunshine I was unable to see her.

Your Fragrant Perfume

Some years ago I was having a conversation with a man who worked for a radio station. We were talking about the context of my books, and he confessed this story.

My daughter was killed a few years ago on July 18. She always wore a musk perfume. I'm a single man, now, and have never dated a lady that wore musk perfume.

Every once in a while, when I'm at home, I can smell that musk perfume, and I know she is here with me. She is one of my guardian angels, and some day I would like to learn how to contact her.

Books by
Ellen Marie Blend

Books of Psychic Phenomena

Visual Encounters

Unraveling The Weave

Looking Back

Conversing on a Higher Level

An Autobiography
(downsizing and discrimination)

Not About Money

Upcoming Books by Ellen Blend

The Educator

Impunity from Lunacy – Book Two

www.ingramcontent.com/pod-product-compliance
Lightning Source LLC
Chambersburg PA
CBHW072003040426
42447CB00009B/1462